THE
PATH
OF
JOY

THE PATH OF JOY

A GUIDE TO CREATING A JOYOUS LIFE

Carla A. Nelson

Library of Congress Catalog Card
Number: 96-90723

ISBN: 0-9655078-0-7

WINDSONG PUBLISHING CO.
P.O. Box 220
Bridgton, Maine 04009

This book is dedicated

to

David

in love and appreciation.

ACKNOWLEDGMENTS

I would like to first and foremost acknowledge and thank my husband, Mel, for his unwavering belief, support and love. I would also like to express my appreciation to Moonyeon Colville, Craig Congleton, David Feinberg, and Ted Godlaski, all of whom have enhanced my life and healing. This book would not have been possible without them.

In addition, I would like to thank Paul Sanders and Sam Quick for their excellent comments and suggestions on the manuscript. Also, special thanks to Patty King and Kathy Brown for their valuable assistance, and to Linda Pugh, Phyllis Bahder and Dixie Badger for believing in me and in my writing.

Finally, my heart-felt appreciation to Genie Dailey for her invaluable contribution to the final creation of this book.

Contents

PROLOGUE

Joy is the birthright of every soul.

This is a small book, a primer to assist you on entering upon the one true Path, the Path of Joy. It is your birthright to live in Joy, to create happiness and fullness in your life. While the steps are simple, and the Path is available to all who are ready to hear the truth of existence on this planet, only those who are willing to do battle with the negative and fearful part of themselves (ego) will benefit from this book. If your ego is as powerful and as dark as mine has been, you will experience strong resistance to beginning the journey, and at times you may have difficulty staying upon the Path. This is no cause for concern, however, for you will be supported in ways you cannot now imagine, and any difficulties experienced will be well worth the struggle.

INTRODUCTION

This book has been brought into existence to bring light to a troubled planet. Its purpose is to enable people to consciously connect with the highest and most loving part of themselves, their Higher Self.

We all have a Higher Self, a highly developed part of our consciousness that is both loving and wise. It is the part of ourselves that loves unconditionally, that sees only the good in us and in everyone else. It is the Christ Spirit within each of us. Higher Self is our closest connection to God, or All That Is. Consciously connecting to Higher Self allows us to change the way we live. We learn to change our unhappy patterns, and to heal ourselves emotionally and spiritually. We learn to live in Joy.

The steps to connect to Higher Self are not difficult, and are described in Chapter 7. We can ask our Higher Self for guidance, and receive it. We can learn to live in Higher Self. We can learn to live in

Joy.

We are living in Higher Self whenever we choose to respond in love — either to ourselves or to others. When we are happy, generous, understanding, caring or genuinely concerned with the well-being of another, we are living in Higher Self. Whenever we respond with wisdom and love to the people and events in our life, we are choosing to align with our Higher Self, and therefore are choosing to live in Joy.

Most of us want to be happy, to live in Joy. Yet the sad truth is that many of us are not happy. Pain permeates our lives. We struggle against the pain, or we try and numb it by engaging in endless activity, or addictive behaviors, refusing to fully face ourselves and our anger and fears. We spend massive amounts of money and time seeking relief from our pain. We exert great effort looking outside ourselves for the magic cure: seeking the 'right' therapist, or relationship, or career, or life change, or drug — or whatever else we believe may help us. Yet the solution is not outside of us, but within.

There is great wisdom within us, and great love. Healing love. Consciously connecting to our Higher Self allows us access to this wisdom and love. Our Higher Self will guide us if we will but ask. We can overcome fear (ego) and embark upon a joyful life path.

It is necessary to point out that the term ego, as used in this book, does not have the same definition as Freud's 'ego', which is popularly used by today's mental health professionals. I have used the word ego to define the fearful part of our personalty that likes us to stay where we are, and that so often controls us. It is the negative voice inside us that is forever judging and scolding. It warns us of scarcity, and the negative intentions of others. Ego is the part of ourselves that tells us we are somehow not good enough, that we do not deserve real happiness, and that we had better maintain the status quo. Ego is our fear, and it often encourages us to remain in unhappy situations or relationships. Ego (fear) can have powerful control of our emotions. Yet ego loses its destructive power in the light and love of our Higher Self.

Because the *The Path Of Joy* is about me and my life, I would like to share how it came into being. I have always considered myself a therapist, not a writer, and it never occurred to me that I would write a book. As a child I was the victim of severe abuse, and I entered adulthood with many emotional scars — plus an overwhelming amount of anger, most of which I took out on myself. For over twenty years I have devoted a large part of my life to healing myself and others. I have tried to recognize and release my negative thoughts and destructive patterns, and I have assisted others to do the same. I have consciously worked at being more loving to myself and to all those in my life. It has been a difficult trek at times, as ego has often overwhelmed me with feelings of hopelessness, despair and fear. Approximately eight years ago I unexpectedly made the connection to my Higher Self, and my life has changed completely since that time.

I am convinced I could never have achieved the deep level of emotional healing and glorious feeling of freedom I now enjoy without the wise and loving guidance I received from my Higher Self. Yet when I was told to write *The Path Of Joy*, I balked. I did not see myself as a writer, and I was not certain I was up to the task. Then the circumstances of my life changed suddenly, and I found myself with the space and time to write. I have had much assistance from my Higher Self, and from my spiritual guides and teachers in writing this book, and it has been a most joyful experience for me. I hope it will be for you as well.

PART ONE

THE PATH OF JOY

1

THE TIME FOR JOY IS NOW

*Joy lifts the heart
and lightens our lives.*

This is a small book with a large message: the time for Joy is NOW. It is essential to the fate of the world that positive changes begin occurring immediately in all areas of life — spiritually, ecologically and personally. The purpose of this book is to teach those who are ready ways to connect with the highest part of themselves in order to bring lasting positive change to their lives.

The Path of Joy is in truth a path of love: love of self and love of all others. It is a gentle path. Following this path allows for a flowering of greater understanding, and therefore greater self-acceptance. All that is required is a willingness to be still and look within, but this willingness takes a great amount of courage. We are so afraid of what we will find. For this reason, most of us spend our lives engaging in endless activity that brings less and less satisfaction as time passes. Our frantic lives become prisons we have created from fear, from our sense of endless obligation to others, and from the demands of our own ego.

We all have ego to contend with. I am defining ego as our fear. It is our mistaken belief about who we really are. At our core, we are all very loving and very good. But our fear (ego) so often gets in the way of our inherent lovingness. Ego is the fearful and negative part of our personality that tells us we are not good enough, that we do not do enough, and that what we do does not really make the grade. Ego is very powerful and clever, and is so often dishonest in what it tells us. This is because ego's primary purpose *is to control our lives.* It usually does this through fear — and there are so many forms of fear. The need to control is fear. Pride is fear. Anger is fear. Self-loathing is fear. Guilt is fear. Punishment of self or others is fear. Lack of love is fear, as is lack of courage. There are many other forms that fear takes. You know them well.

We often unwittingly allow ego to run our lives, which is unfortunate, because *the job of ego is to stop Joy*. Left unbridled, ego invariably leads to loss of Joy. Our greatest suffering occurs not from others, but from within ourselves. We are so often our own worst enemy. The unhappy and critical voice we hear reminding us of our mistakes and shortcomings, telling us happiness cannot last, warning us of scarcity or the negative intentions of others, is always ego. And ego is *insane*, because the messages it gives us are irrational and unloving. Yet we rarely question the beliefs of our ego, or the messages we receive from it. I tell you this because your ego will be the one great obstacle to beginning — and remaining — upon the Path of Joy.

Yet ego is powerless in the light of love, for there it can be seen and transformed. Those who truly seek a happier and more loving life will receive all the support necessary, often from unanticipated sources. But it is from the highest part of each person that the greatest support will emerge. We all have this higher part, this Higher Self within us. And if we will only slow down and clear our minds, this higher source of love and wisdom can be tapped into at will, supplying us with wise counsel and loving guidance for our lives. It is like having access to a very wise Being who loves you unconditionally, and who is there to offer assistance whenever needed. Once you connect to your Higher Self, you need never feel alone, for you can call upon this higher part of yourself whenever you desire guid-ance or support. It is a marvelous blessing and is available to all who seek the Path of Joy.

2

WHAT IS THE PATH OF JOY ?

*Joy is the normal
result of a love-filled life.*

The Path of Joy is a path of love — love of self and love of others. It is choosing to create a life that brings true contentment and satisfaction. When we experience genuine happiness or delight, it can be said we are in a state of Joy. It is during those moments when we are doing something loving or positive that we most often experience Joy.

Because the Path of Joy is the path of love, it requires that we make a conscious choice to learn to love. Learning to love encompasses many things. You begin *with yourself* by making a conscious commitment to self-healing, which includes the following:

(1) **You must be willing to challenge and**

23

eliminate the negative and unloving messages you give yourself. I suggest you begin by making the commitment to write down every critical or judgmental thought you have about yourself for just one day, beginning when you get up in the morning and continuing until you are ready to fall asleep. I think you will be amazed at the volume of negative self-talk you are feeding yourself. These unloving messages include: blaming yourself, negatively comparing yourself with others, not feeling adequate, envying someone else, putting yourself down (for example, thinking 'I never do anything right'), not feeling attractive, or competent, or lovable, or needed — the list goes on and on. Most of us judge ourselves so harshly that self-love seems impossible.

You *can* learn to love yourself. Now is the time to stop the negative self-talk, and begin consciously giving yourself loving messages. Tell yourself, "I am wonderful!" You are, whether you believe it now or not. Tell yourself you are loving, intelligent, and competent. And most of all, tell yourself you are *worthy* of love and Joy, for you truly are, regardless of the mistakes you have made in your life.

As you begin to eliminate the harsh 'judge' inside yourself, which in reality is your fear (ego), you will become more loving not only to yourself, but to everyone in your life. And this will bring you Joy.

(2) **In order to achieve self-healing, you**

must be willing to make loving changes in some of the ways you think and act. You cannot continue self-limiting thoughts and behaviors if you want to walk the Path of Joy. Seeing yourself as less than you are (and most of us do) creates feelings of powerlessness and hopelessness. Believing you are not talented enough, or educated enough, or smart enough, or worthy enough to go after what you truly want and need creates a victim mentality. And we all know what victims do: they give away their power.

Choosing the Path of Joy requires taking back your power, and giving up all thoughts and behaviors that limit or demean you. I have learned from working with many people as a therapist that no one is any stronger or any weaker than anyone else. You have the power and strength within you to change your life. That is a given. The question you must ask yourself is, "Am I willing to utilize my power?" Are you willing to be loyal and truthful to yourself, and honor the unique person that you are? Self-healing cannot occur until you make the choice to love and honor the matchless individual that is you.

(3) **The process of healing yourself requires a willingness to give up the familiar (and often comfortable) misery of your life, and choosing instead to practice living in Joy.** What

this really means is assuming total responsibility for your life, and the way you live it. You must choose to look at the parts of your life that are not working well, and decide to make positive changes. The changes may be as simple as changing your poor eating habits or learning to say 'no' to others' unreasonable demands of you. But at times it may require making dramatic changes in your life. You may have to leave people or situations that are destructive and unloving to you.

What I sadly have discovered is that so many people prefer the known misery of their lives to facing the unknown. Knowing how to end your suffering does not necessarily mean you will choose to do so. But do so you must, if you want to walk the Path of Joy — for suffering is incompatible with Joy.

Those who choose to change their lives to one of love and Joy will benefit greatly from connecting to Higher Self. I have assisted many people in connecting with their Higher Self and I can teach you if you are ready and willing. That part is not difficult. What is difficult is taking the risk to make positive changes in your life. Your Higher Self can guide you in seeing the Path, but only you can make the choice to walk it. The guidance you receive will be gentle and loving, and will help you to shine light upon the dark areas in your life. But sometimes this is painful, and sometimes we do not want to see the truth.

For example, a woman may want to follow the Path of Joy until it becomes apparent she can only continue on the Path if she leaves her emotionally abusive partner. While she realizes he often brings her down with his cutting remarks (that mirror the words of her ego), she may not want to give him up. Why? Because how can she be certain she will find someone else? She may decide to stop listening to her Higher Self and stay with her partner, because misery can seem safer than facing the unknown. And once she stops seeking, and stops listening, she is off the Path, and her life continues to be unsatisfying and joyless. Yet if she listens to what she knows is the truth, and summons up the courage to release her partner from her life in love for them both, she will open up space that can be filled with people who affirm her and bring her Joy.

Following the Path of Joy never calls for sacrifice, but at times it does require releasing from our lives people or situations that no longer serve our higher purpose. And while this may require great courage, the result is always increased Joy.

3

PRINCIPLES OF THE PATH OF JOY

*Love is the answer to
every question and the
solution to all unhappiness.*

We begin on the Path of Joy the moment we decide love is the answer to every question and the solution to ending all our unhappiness. It is a very simple truth that you get from life exactly what you give. Give love, and you receive love. The more you are able to express and receive love, the more Joy you will experience in your life.

The Path of Joy embodies six important principles. Understanding and following these principles will enable you to make whatever changes are necessary to live in Joy.

29

Principle One

The Path of Joy is a Path of Love

We all must choose the path we will walk in life. What path have you chosen? Are you happy? Do you feel Joy? Is your life satisfying and full?

In order to fully enter upon a joyful path, we must be willing to look honestly at ourselves and the lives we have created. For whether we want to believe it or not, the truth is each of us has created the life we are living. We often feel others are the reason for our unhappiness, and that we are victims with little choice or power. This simply is not true. As a therapist I can tell you healing does not occur until such time as we accept full responsibility for our lives, and become willing to make the changes necessary for ending our suffering.

In order to begin walking the Path of Joy, we must be willing to change our life to one of love. This love must begin with ourselves, for we can love others only to the extent that we are able to love ourselves. Have you noticed how much happiness you feel when you treat yourself, or another person, with love and genuine respect? And have you noticed how unhappy you become when you respond in anger or fear to yourself or to someone else?

The Path of Joy requires making a conscious commitment to living a life of love. We must practice loving kindness to ourselves and to everyone who is in our lives. Do you respect and reward yourself for doing the best you can, each and every day? You deserve to be treated with loving kindness at all times, particularly from yourself.

Stop for a moment now and ask: "How do I show love for myself? What are the things I do that show I love and value *me*?" Be precise, and be honest. What do you do that demonstrates you love the person that is you? Take time to really think about this, because this is where one must begin the process of self-healing.

It is regrettable how often we do not act in love for ourselves. We are frequently impatient and judgmental with the person who we most need as our best friend — ourself. In reality, you need kindness and consideration from yourself more than you ever will need it from another. And the more you can love yourself, the more you will be able to love those around you, even the people you now dislike. The Path of Joy requires the willingness to move forward into a more loving way of living our lives. We begin where we are, using the strengths we already have, to start changing the ways we think and act. As we practice treating ourselves with kindness, we learn to respect — and reward — ourselves for doing the best we can, each and every day.

We are all capable of choosing Joy and we are

all capable of learning to love ourselves, regardless of our past mistakes and present self-image. It does not matter how you feel about yourself now, or whether you love yourself or not. All that is necessary is deciding today that you will live your life in love. From that decision, you will begin to see the beauty of who you are as you open your heart to all the love that is within you. And as the flower of your love unfolds, you will recognize your great worth — and you will change your life to Joy.

Principle Two

The Path of Joy is Choosing to Live in Light Rather Than in Darkness

Throughout our lives it seems we are assailed by the negativity and darkness of others. Yet I have come to believe it is our *own* negativity and darkness that creates the vast majority of our suffering. Even when it appears that someone else is causing our pain, most often what is happening is that our own negative beliefs about ourselves are being reflected back to us. Others act as mirrors, for what we see in another is so often within ourselves. This can be a difficult truth to accept.

When I talk of living in darkness, I am referring to the fear, doubt and pain that permeates so many lives. Most of us have so much fear and doubt, and who among us is a stranger to pain? Yet when fear and doubt reign, Joy disappears.

Light is the intelligence of love and compassion. Love and compassion *are* Joy. When we consciously choose to live in light, rather than darkness, a wonderful thing happens. We begin to realize our great power. We realize we actually have the power within us to dispel the darkness in our lives.

I have worked with many people who have suffered abuse as infants and children, as did I. I have seen these courageous souls heal themselves completely by their commitment to transform the darkness within themselves to love and light. They have transcended the darkness of their unhappy pasts by facing the anger and pain within themselves, and choosing to let it go. This is not easy, and it takes time and courage. When dealing with severe abuse, it is often helpful to engage the services of a competent professional who can offer support and direction as the unhappy past is left behind.

Even those fortunate people who have enjoyed relatively happy childhoods must make the choice between living in light or living in darkness, for nobody survives childhood and adolescence unscathed. We all carry scars and we all carry fear. I have yet to meet anyone who does not have anger and pain inside. It is simply the human condition. Life is often difficult, and disappointment abounds, but if we make the choice to live in love, there is ultimately nothing that can prevent our living in Joy.

Principle Three

The Path of Joy Requires Courage

Choosing to live in Joy requires courage, for most of us are not used to living in light, and darkness can feel quite comfortable. Our pain and fear may become so familiar to us that an illusion of safety is created. For example, a man may be unhappy working in a boring, dead-end job, but may stay because he believes it is safe. His job is secure, and if he maintains status quo he will not have to seek other employment or prove his competency in another organization. So he stays, even though he finds it increasingly more difficult to drag himself to the office each day. We often choose what seems safe over what we really want, and in the process sabotage our creativity, our personal power and our Joy.

Living a joyful life requires taking full responsibility for meeting our own needs. It takes the courage to be willing to give up the illusion of safety we have created by playing it safe. We must be willing to live our own truth, whatever that truth is for us. We cannot allow others to control our lives, nor can we continue to stay in situations or relationships that stifle our sense of self or diminish our Joy. There may be times when we will need to make important changes in our lives. Yet change can make us very uncomfortable, and too often we choose to stay where we are, not because we are happy, but because it feels safe. We may avoid making necessary changes because we are afraid. Yet the truth is we can transform our lives to Joy if we will but gather the courage to do so.

Principle Four

The Path of Joy Requires Changing Our Unloving Patterns

In order to walk the Path of Joy, we must be willing to eliminate our unloving patterns from our lives. We must practice self-love, and we must learn to relate to others with kindness and consideration.

When we honestly assess our lives and how we are living them we may be amazed at the many negative patterns we have developed. Do any of the following apply to you?

Refusing to rest, even when tired.

Eating a lot of junk food.

Letting others step on your toes, and saying nothing.

Allowing others to make decisions for you.

Being a workaholic.

Drinking too much.
Using drugs.
Burying your feelings of anger and
resentment inside.
Being a martyr by putting everyone
else's needs above your own.
Sabotaging your success.
Staying in a job you hate.
Staying in an unhappy or destructive
relationship.
Beating yourself up for each mistake,
large or small.
Never taking a chance.
Being afraid to make changes.
Criticizing others.
Criticizing yourself.
Blaming others.
Blaming yourself.
Envying others.
Feeling responsible for others.
Comparing yourself with others.
Never taking a vacation.
Trying to control others.
Judging others.
Judging yourself.
Never varying your routine.
Staying constantly busy.
Trying to be perfect.

Of course, this is only a partial list. Most of us are quite skilled at creating negative and unloving habits, and it takes practice to eliminate them from our lives. It requires being mindful of our thoughts and actions and paying careful attention to how we think and act. We must practice loving ourselves and all others — all of the time. And we must not judge ourselves when we fall back into negative, old patterns, but instead congratulate ourselves on our increased awareness, and then promptly return to a position of love.

Changing our unloving patterns does not need to be difficult. When we make a mistake, or when we react from fear to ourself or another, all that is necessary is to *recognize* our error, and lovingly correct it. For example, if you have hurt someone's feelings, or said unkind words, apologize to them and ask for their forgiveness.

Principle Five

The Path of Joy Requires Willingness To Confront Our Fear

In order to walk the Path of Joy, we must be determined to confront and overcome the fearful and unloving part of ourselves — our ego. This is a formidable task, for most of us have a powerful ego. Much of our lives are lived from fear (ego). In truth there are but two basic emotions: love and fear. Love is from the highest part of ourself. Fear is from our ego. At any given moment in time we must choose which of these emotions will dominate. Will we respond to whatever is occurring from love, or from fear?

For many of us, fear often predominates, and we find ourselves reacting from our fearful ego, rather than responding from love. Fear takes many forms, some of which are mistrust, suspicion, anxiety, jealousy, resentment, doubt, cowardice, nervousness, and panic. There are others, of course. For example, when we feel intimidated by someone, we are in fear, and we are also reacting from fear whenever we attempt to intimidate, manipulate or control another. We are in fear when we experience self-doubt or self-loathing, or when we suffer feelings of worry or care. Whenever we feel frightened about anything, or *whenever we are angry,* we are in fear. And whenever we are in fear, we are in ego. Since fear is the opposite of love, it is very difficult to respond in a loving way to anyone (including ourselves) when we are experiencing fear in any form.

The fearful part of ourselves, our ego, is so often in control of our lives, creating unhappiness and sorrow. We must be willing to look within ourselves and begin to honestly confront our fear. Only then can we replace our fearful reactions with loving responses, and begin living in Joy.

Principle Six

The Path of Joy Is Choosing To Live Joyously

Electing to live in Joy requires full acceptance of two important truths. The first truth is *we create our own lives.* The second truth is *Joy is our birthright.*

We are the authors of our lives. My life is my creation, and your life is your creation. At any given moment in time we are choosing the way we will live our lives. I did not always believe this truth. For many years I thought I had no choice about many of the things that happened in my life, and I felt victimized and resentful. Now that I am in my fifties I look back and realize that since reaching adulthood *I have always been at choice.* I have never been a victim, for there was nothing that happened to me that I did not choose somehow. Nothing. While I did not consciously decide to have unpleasant and negative experiences, I now know that these experiences could not have happened without my consent.

Let me share an example. For many years I felt devalued and unappreciated by some of the most significant women in my life. I believed I gave much more energy and love to them than they gave to me. It took me years to realize I was choosing to focus my attention on them, rather than on myself. I was looking for them to love and validate me, and when they did not, I felt hurt and resentful. I finally learned only I could validate me, and I began focusing my attention and love on myself. That took pressure off those who did love me, and our relationships became more mutually satisfying. The women who were only interested in a one-sided relationship decided to look elsewhere, and I no longer had to deal with them. I now attract loving women into my life who give as well as receive.

Numerous people come for therapy who truly believe they are powerless. They feel like victims of fate, or they feel victimized by other people. Many believe they have to put up with unloving behaviors (from mates, children, parents, co-workers, etc.). Others deprive themselves of happiness by following unhappy old scripts. We so often do things we do not want to do because we believe we *have* to do them, or at the very least, we *should* do them. Fear traps many people in unhappy situations that could be changed. We do create our lives. Accepting this truth fully will empower you to change your life in any way you choose. You can create a more joyous life if you truly decide to do so.

The second truth we must learn is that Joy is

our birthright. We have the right to be happy. More than that, it is the will of our Higher Self that we be happy. Most of us want to be happy, and work diligently at attaining happiness. The problem is we are looking for happiness in all the wrong places. We forget that there is nothing outside ourselves that can bring lasting Joy or contentment. Nothing. Yet we continue to desperately seek, and invariably wind up feeling disappointed when we realize that what we thought would make us happy does not.

Seeking happiness outside of yourself is as much a waste of time as searching for the Fountain of Youth. You are not going to find either one. But learning to focus love and kindness on yourself will enable you to make the changes that are needed to create a more joyous life. Treat yourself as you would your dearest, most valued friend. Make time every day to do something you truly enjoy, regardless of how 'busy' you are. Learn to fill your own cup rather than waiting for others to do it for you. Begin now to nurture yourself. And most important of all, take the time to look within, so that you can begin to discover the wisest and most loving part of yourself — your Higher Self.

4

CHOOSING TO CONNECT TO HIGHER SELF

*Fear decreases and Joy
increases as we listen to the
wise and loving voice within.*

Why might one choose to connect with their Higher Self? There are many reasons, but perhaps the most common one is the desire to heal emotionally and grow spiritually, in order to create a happier, more satisfying life.

My initial connection with my Higher Self occurred most unexpectedly, during a time when my life was not working as I wanted it to. My relationship with my teenage daughter was conflictive and disappointing. She was an excellent student and had many friends, but at home she was angry and rebellious. There seemed to be almost constant conflict between us, and I did not know how to change our unhappy patterns. In addition, the memories of a very abusive and unhappy childhood kept surfacing, contaminating my current life. I was unhappy and did not know how to deal with all the feelings I was experiencing. I was a therapist helping others work through their problems, and was also in therapy trying to work through my own.

The connection to my Higher Self occurred during this difficult time. My therapist had been encouraging me to vent my angry feelings in a letter to my parents, which was then to be destroyed. For months I had resisted this, although I often used this technique with my own clients. (Therapists often make difficult clients!) One day I was feeling particularly awful, and I finally sat down and wrote a scathing, anger-filled letter to my parents. When I was finished with the letter, I cried for a long time, allowing myself to release much anger and pain.

Then, to my great surprise, I heard a quiet voice within me that seemed to be coming from a different part of myself, a higher and more loving part. The voice was gentle and wise. I picked up my pen and wrote down what I was hearing, *"Carla, I am your Higher Self — your real self — the one you have kept hidden. I am now coming out of the closet, so to speak, and am planning on taking my rightful place as head of your personality.*

"It is time to let the past go. You are gaining nothing except misery by holding on to such a dreary past. The present is really very much okay — very satisfactory — if only you would wake up and look. IT IS TIME TO WAKE UP NOW.

"Carla, you are really quite adequate. Give up refusing to see who you are. You won't like to hear this, but it is time to forgive your parents. Let the anger and hurt go. They are insignificant in your life and you can afford to be generous. Don't let them in, but let the hurt out. Then you can forgive and be free.

"You are very loving. Start now to love yourself. Treat yourself with kindness and consideration. Eat right and get enough exercise. I am always with you, and love you more than you can know."

After reading the message I had received, I became very concerned. I had heard a voice! What did that say about my mental state? I had always led a conservative life, and nothing like this had ever happened to me before, or to anyone I knew. I had absolutely no idea what 'Higher Self' meant. But I could not deny that I had heard a voice. To say I felt upset would be a definite understatement.

Early the next morning as I was sitting quietly I heard the voice again, *"Good morning, Carla! The start of another new day. It promises to be a beauti-*

ful one. You know who I am. I am your Higher Self. In reality I am the one true Carla. Today we will begin letting go of the past. We will do this by first noticing what a beautiful day it is. Look outside, see the trees, how beautiful and green everything is. Look at your cat and dog — how perfect they are, how complete. And so are you. I know you don't believe this yet, but you are whole and complete, and in no way defective. It is an insult to me to ever see yourself as less than what you are — I create only perfection. I, however, never feel 'insulted', only sad when a perfect creation refuses to recognize itself. Inevitably, they will, each and every one.

"Taste your coffee. Really taste it. Breathe deeply. It will take some practice to change your thought patterns, and some struggle. I love you and will become more and more a part of your life. Be not afraid. You will not lose Carla in the process, but will find yourself instead. I am with you always and forever."

The next day I received another message, *"Enjoy the gift of your animals. These things will pass and will seem to be taken from you, but not really. Everything God created continues forever, including Cupcake and Maxim* (my aged cat and dog). *You cannot really lose them.*

"All there is is love — nothing else is real. Love yourself, Carla, that is my commandment to you. Continue to take good care of yourself and teach oth-

ers to do the same. *I want you to be happy, now and always."*

I asked about my parents and received this answer, *"Do not let them in emotionally, but try to love them, and pray for them always. Put light around them in your mind. There is incredible power in love."*

After meditating the next day, I heard the voice again. The message received was helpful and wise, and ended with, *"Be not afraid, either of me or of yourself. There is nothing to fear. Much joy and peace lie ahead for you. You are coming home to me, where you have yearned to return. You fear you will lose yourself, but that cannot happen. It is not my will for you to lose yourself, but rather to find yourself. You are now in the process of doing that. Rejoice and be of good cheer. Enjoy this special day and remember I am with you always."*

Although I was intrigued by the messages I was receiving, I was concerned I might be losing touch with reality. It all seemed so strange, and it made *me* feel strange. Was I losing my sanity?

The next day as I sat quietly, the voice appeared in my mind again, saying, *"Good morning, Carla. Another beautiful day! Hear the birds singing — and the day is fresh and new.*

"You are not 'losing it'. This brings us to your real fear of being crazy. Another ploy of the ego, for you can never be crazy following me. I teach only

truth, peace, happiness and love.

"Your anger continues to surface, doesn't it, but at a more manageable level. Continue to allow it to come — and let it go. You are freeing yourself from the bondage of your self-made prison. All is well..... Carla, be happy. Continue to take care of your body, and practice loving yourself more and more. As you learn to love yourself, you will also love others. Continue on your path with faith and happiness. I am always with you."

That same day I saw my therapist. With great trepidation, I showed him my 'writings'. To my relief, he assured me I was not crazy, and told me to keep writing. I will always be grateful to him for his encouragement, and also for my husband's support, for at times I felt very uncomfortable doing this. Nevertheless, I continued to listen and to write what I heard. And always the guidance was wise, or as my therapist would tell me, "right on target". I was helped to reach a deeper level of therapy, and my healing progressed at a rapid rate.

With the guidance of my Higher Self, I was able to look at the pain and darkness within myself, which could then be recognized and released. I was lovingly helped to see my errors and the destructive patterns in my life. I had to honestly face my anger, resentment and fear, and recognize how these negative emotions had kept me from living in Joy.

Seeing all of this was often very painful, but as I allowed myself to face each demon within, I was able to let them go. I was helped to recognize my mistakes and the errors in my thinking, and that allowed me conscious choice. I could correct my patterns or stay where I was. Since I was not satisfied where I was, I usually chose the path of change, although this was often very frightening. And with each change, and each small correction in my thinking, my happiness increased, and I felt lighter.

Following the guidance of my Higher Self has consistently released me from emotional pain and fear (ego) and has increased my Joy. Yet there are times I refuse to listen, preferring to stay where I am for a while. The voice remains gentle and loving and the guidance continues.

5

SELF-LOVE

*Let each heart be filled
with love, for love begets
Joy. In truth, love is Joy.*

There are few of us who have not at one time or another asked the age-old questions: "Why am I here?" "What is the purpose of my life?" During times of great uncertainty, stress or despair, it is natural to wonder what the purpose of life really is. That we are here on planet Earth is obvious, but *why*?

For many years I struggled to understand the meaning of life in general, and my life in particular. There were times that were so difficult I questioned whether there was any purpose to life at all. It was not until I began to practice self-love that I realized what life is truly all about. Life is about love. *We are here to learn to love.* This is the purpose of my life, and it is the purpose of yours. Nothing else brings any lasting satisfaction or Joy. You can attain everything the world has to offer, but if your life is loveless, genuine happiness will forever elude you.

The most important person to learn to love is *you*. Contrary to what many of us have been taught, loving ourselves is not selfish or wrong. When we truly learn self-love, a wonderful thing happens: our love of others increases. We find ourselves becoming kinder and more considerate to everyone we come in contact with. Our relationships improve, and our Joy increases.

Self-love is the process of learning who you really are. It is in reality a stripping away of all that is not you. Your fear (ego) is not you; it is not who you are. Your accomplishments and perceived failures are not you. Your mistakes are not you. Your possessions are not you; your children are not you; and your social status is not you. Your body is not you — it is not who you really are (you are much, much more than a body). You are in essence love and light. And so is everyone else. You, like all others, are here to learn who you are. This learning can most easily be accomplished in Joy, and can only occur through the process of self-love.

Self-love seems so very difficult to achieve, but

in truth it is not. All that is required is a strong desire to be more loving, and a willingness to manifest this increased lovingness in all areas of your life. *It must begin with you.*

The process of learning to love yourself begins with the basics: taking care of your physical body; healing your mind; and developing greater spiritual awareness. I will discuss each of these now.

Taking Care Of Your Body

While it is true your body is not who you really are, it is also true you cannot get by without it! Because your body is essential to your life, it deserves love and care.

You take care of your body by eating healthy foods, and by avoiding unhealthy ones. It is difficult to develop greater self-love when you eat mostly junk food and deprive your body of needed nutrients, or if you drink too much, use drugs, or engage in compulsive behaviors. Addictions decrease self-love, whether it be a food addiction, a gambling or drug addiction, a sexual addiction — or any other kind of addiction. It is necessary to put the body in healthy balance by developing proper eating habits, getting regular exercise, avoiding toxic substances or activities, and getting enough rest. Treat your body with love and respect, and see how much better it performs for you.

Healing Your Mind

Healing the mind is a necessary component in increasing self-love. *You begin healing your mind when you choose to take full responsibility for your life.* Very few of us want to do this, it seems. We often prefer to live in unhappiness and put the blame on someone or something else: "If only my husband would stop drinking, then I would be happy," or "if only my wife were more affectionate," or "if only my daughter would choose better friends," or "if only I had more money, or were more beautiful, or had a better job." The list goes on and on. We so often think that if others treated us more lovingly we would be happier. *But the truth is that only by treating ourselves more lovingly can we escape the unhappiness of our lives and experience Joy.*

It is amazing how reluctant we can be to changing our unloving patterns towards ourselves. For many of us, it seems easier to be loving and generous to others, rather than to ourselves. Yet we can love others only to the extent that we can love ourselves, and often our gifts of love to others are in reality attempts on our part to get them to love us. And even when they *do* love us, so often there is still this awful emptiness within. This emptiness can only be filled by us. You must be willing to accept this truth. Only you can fill the emptiness within, and it can only be filled by your loving yourself.

The decision to accept full responsibility for your life and happiness includes being willing to own your feelings — all of them. Even the ugly ones. It has been my experience as a therapist that most of us are willing to face our hurt, sadness and disappointment, but we are much more reluctant to face our anger and rage. Yet healing simply cannot occur unless we are willing to face our own darkness. When we admit we are angry, when we acknowledge our rage, it brings these feelings to a conscious level of awareness. We then can choose to release these feelings.

Fear is the reason many of us are reluctant to feel and express negative emotions. We may believe it is wrong to be angry, and that feeling rage makes us a terrible person. Or we may fear being punished for having 'bad' feelings. Many of my clients have expressed the fear that if they began feeling their angry feelings, they might become completely overwhelmed by them. We can become so afraid of our own anger, resentment and rage that we turn these feelings inside, because they are unacceptable to us. We forget that feelings are only feelings — they are not who we are. Holding negative feelings inside is a mistake, for left unresolved they literally can make us ill — and often do. When we have the courage to feel our anger and our pain, we find we are able to release these feelings. We do not stay stuck in them.

There are many safe ways to release negative feelings that have been kept bottled up. A common therapeutic technique is to write an angry letter to whoever you are angry at, even if that person is yourself. Make the letter as honest and as angry as you can, writing whatever it is you feel, even if you feel guilty for doing so. I encourage my clients to put as much rage into the letter as possible. After the letter is finished, destroy it. Tear it up into little pieces or burn it. Doing this helps release these feelings.

Another effective way to clear anger and pain from within yourself is to keep an anger journal. Simply buy a tablet, and begin writing your negative feelings down. Allow yourself to really feel the sadness, pain, resentment and anger you have been holding inside. Do not leave anyone out. Feel and express your honest emotions about whoever has hurt you in your life, and do not hold back. Let the feelings out, and honor these feelings by not judging them, or yourself for having them. You have a right to your feelings. Anger is not bad, as so many of us have been taught.

In my life, my anger has served to protect me,

for it forced me to look at my life and the way I was living it. Not only was I often unloving to myself, I also allowed others to be unloving to me as well. (People generally treat us the same way we treat ourselves.) Facing my anger allowed me to see the changes I needed to make in my life — and helped empower me to make them. When we are truly angry, hurt or resentful, there is usually a valid reason for the way we are feeling. Anger functions as a safeguard in our lives, and we ignore it at our peril.

Engaging in physical exercise is another safe way to get rid of negative emotions. Chopping wood, jogging, and vigorous swimming help to release unwanted and unhappy feelings, as does taking long walks. I had a client who discovered a safe and creative way to release his pent-up rage at his boss. He was an avid golfer, and he had his boss's name printed on some of his golf balls. He told me he released a lot of anger hitting those golf balls!

Sitting alone and screaming can quickly release negative feelings, as can beating on a pillow. Allow the feelings to come. Do not be afraid of them, for they are only feelings. If you feel you may lose control of yourself, work with a trusted friend, or seek the assistance of a competent therapist. There is no reason you have to carry around emotional garbage, for doing so prohibits living in Joy.

It takes courage to face the darkness within, but

doing so allows us to recognize our demons, and to let them go. This clears the mind, and allows for a lightening of our emotional state. We can then fill our minds with more loving emotions and thoughts, and greatly increase our level of Joy.

In addition to clearing out pain, anger and old resentments, it is necessary to recognize the way our fear (ego) controls us. This often takes the most courage of all, for ego controls through fear. A favorite control method of my ego has been guilt. In the past, I would become emotionally paralyzed by feelings of guilt, which usually manifested themselves as feeling overly responsible for others. I felt responsible for my children, my clients, my siblings, and my friends. I felt responsible for nearly everybody in my life. I truly believed it was my duty to put everyone else first. It was a very heavy burden to carry, and I often felt angry and resentful, because it seemed nobody was feeling responsible for me. (When we put ourselves last, so does everyone else.)

Confronting my ego's belief that my only self-worth came from taking care of others was difficult, and it had to be done many, many times. Changing the old patterns was frightening, for I had to endure powerful feelings of guilt when I chose to honor myself, rather than trying to please someone else. I continued to face my anger and resentment as I struggled to be less responsible for others and more responsible for myself. And through it all I was supported by loving guidance from my Higher Self. I was encouraged to feel my rage and resentment, and to release these feelings. I was gently told to practice loving myself.

Among the many messages I received were the following: *"Carla, your lesson to be learned is self-love, and freedom from feeling responsible for others. When you feel responsible for others, you slow yourself down, and them as well.*

"You are always afraid. Challenge your fears, for all are irrational. You fear most of all not being perfect. Perfect is not of this world. It is unreasonable and unloving of you to expect this from yourself.

"There is only learning in this world, so ultimately, what is there to fear? Release yourself from your search for perfection, and release yourself from your search for 'happiness', and you will be free. There will no longer be the anxiety and fear within you. Seeking happiness from outside of yourself is a waste of time, and so is feeling responsible for others.

"Give love — give always from love. Never give from feelings of responsibility. There is no need to feel responsible for other adults, as each soul has chosen for itself its path, and you have no power or control over that. This includes your grown children.

"Practice self-love. This, of course, always leads to love of others."

And another message regarding my children: *"In truth there is only one thing you are responsible for in regards to your grown children, and that is to see them as competent adults, and to speak only words of love and affirmation to them. That is all you are responsible for, Dearest Carla. And this is truth.*

"You are not responsible for cooking for them, or entertaining them, or supporting them financially (although financial gifts of love are fine if not over-done), or subjugating your wants and needs and desires to their wants and needs and desires. You are responsible for your Joy and they are respon-sible for their own. And this is truth. You speak lov-ingly to them and you affirm their great worth by your unconditional love of them. That is all. And while they are visiting you, (my children were com-ing for the Christmas holiday) *remember that your responsibility is to yourself, to treat yourself with great consideration and love. Allow yourself to sim-ply be, and to concentrate on meeting your own needs. This is not selfish or wrong, and is in truth the lov-ing thing for your children as well."*

And another message regarding self-love: *"You are here to learn how to love better, both yourself and all others. By acting in love for yourself, you will be acting in love for others."*

"It is necessary to realize acting in love comes from the higher part of yourself. It does not mean self-indulgence or lack of concern for others. To the contrary, when you act in love for yourself, you cease destructive patterns with others, and this is loving for all concerned.

"Doing the loving thing for yourself sometimes takes great courage. Be very patient and gentle with yourself as you practice self-love, as you begin changing your unloving patterns to yourself.

"The result of all of this is increased freedom, increased Joy, and increased intimacy with others who are loving."

Healing the mind is an ongoing process and happens more easily and gently when done in Joy. We are here to learn. We can learn through pain and suffering, or we can learn through Joy. Either way we are continually learning. After many years of pain and struggle, I now prefer to learn my lessons in a more gentle way. And I finally realize that feeling overly responsible for others is a dead-end street, and that searching for happiness outside of myself is not nearly as satisfying as living in Joy.

Developing Greater Spiritual Awareness

The process of developing greater spiritual awareness is not difficult, and is in truth a most joyful endeavor. All that is required is a deep longing for connectedness to God, or All That Is. You must be willing to go within yourself and find the connection to God, or to your Higher Power, that is already there. This necessitates an expansion in the way you view yourself, which can occur quickly, or develop slowly. It does not matter.

We seem to fear looking deep within ourselves, afraid of what we will find. Yet what we find is *really very glorious*, for what we find is our connectedness to God. And we also discover in the process that at our core we are quite wonderful, and that we possess a marvelous capacity for love and Joy. When we strip away the hurt, fear, sadness and anger that has enveloped us like black fog, we begin to see the wonderful light of our Soul. And this is joyous indeed. To begin this wonderful process, we must make a serious and conscious commitment to increasing our spiritual awareness. There is no quick fix. We must be willing to make the time available for the process to unfold.

I have discovered that it is necessary for me, and for many people I have worked with, to set aside a certain time each day for meditative reflection. It is helpful to begin by calming and relaxing the mind and body, and it is necessary to find what works best for you. Some people find it helpful to listen to beautiful, soothing music. Others read from the

Bible or other inspiring books. Many people relax their mind by reading daily meditations or affirmations. For me, sitting quietly for a few minutes and going within myself helps me to calm my mind and get centered. Find a special place where you can be alone and not be interrupted.

Making time every day for quiet reflection speeds up the process of developing greater spiritual awareness, for it is in these quiet moments when we are alone with ourselves that many insights occur. Often we discover answers to questions and solutions to problems that have plagued us for years. And it is in these quiet moments we begin to truly get to know ourselves — to discover who we really are.

Do not be afraid to be alone with yourself. Make the time to get to know who you truly are. You will be pleasantly surprised by the wellspring of love and wisdom that is within you. Do not make the mistake of thinking you are your feelings and emotions, for you are not. You possess great love and great power. This is truth. You will find your Higher Self if you but ask. And your Higher Self is who you really are.

Increasing Self-Love

Several years ago, after clearing my mind, I began a morning meditation by asking the following question: "How can I increase my self-love?"

I immediately received the following message: *"You ask how you can increase your self-love, and I will tell you. You begin with accepting who you are. You are a loving being of light. That is who you are. All else falls away when this simple truth is recognized.*

"Secondly, you practice love of self by realizing there is a loving Universe which gently orchestrates your life on earth. Surrender in Joy to your life experiences, remembering always to act in love at all times.

"You increase self-love when you refrain from accepting the expectations of the world, and instead accept the expectations of the Universe. Worldly successes and pleasures bring no lasting Joy. Living in love does, for living in love is living in Joy.

"Treat yourself with loving respect.

"Treat others with loving respect.

"Release anger and negativity by accepting the feelings, and making the choice to let these feelings go.

"Take every opportunity to practice Joy. Take walks. Watch sunsets. Listen to music. Draw. Sculpt. Work in your garden. Love your pets. Enjoy children. Forgive yourself. Forgive others. Remember, you are here to learn and to love. Congratulate yourself for all you have learned and all you are learning. Trust

yourself. Cease striving for perfection, for it is not possible here. Accept who you are now, for you are wonderful. Remember that truth, and live it.

"What I have said is truth for you, and all others."

PART TWO

CONNECTING WITH

HIGHER SELF

6

REWARDS OF CONNECTING WITH
HIGHER SELF

*Seek deeply within
yourself, for there lie
the answers to all questions.*

It has been many years since I first discovered my Higher Self. Until that time, I did not realize there was such a thing as a Higher Self, and it took several years before I felt comfortable telling others about my experience. Yet from the very beginning, I could not deny the fact that the guidance I was receiving was greatly enhancing both my healing and my life. As time passed, I came to realize more and more how fortunate I was to have access to this wise and loving part of myself. Connecting with my Higher Self has been the greatest blessing of my life. You, too, have a Higher Self, and I want to share this blessing with you.

Following the loving and wise guidance of my Higher Self has changed my life in so many ways. I am no longer angry at anyone, not even at me. I used to have so much anger inside me that at times I thought I might blow up into a million pieces (like Mt. St. Helens!). Now the anger is gone, and I am free of the hold it had over me. I still get angry at times, but when I do there is much less emotional charge, and the anger is centered in the present. I am more patient and loving with others, because I have learned to be more patient and loving with me. I do not feel I have to be perfect any more, nor do I expect others to be perfect. It feels very liberating.

When problems arise, I make time to connect with my Higher Self and ask for guidance. When I do not know how to respond to a person or a situation, I ask that my higher purpose be explained to me, so that I can do the loving thing for myself — and whoever else is involved. I do not always like the messages I receive, because there are times I must admit that the error is my own, and I need to correct my thinking. Yet when I make the necessary changes, peace and Joy return to my life.

I am not the only one whose life has benefited

from making the connection to Higher Self. There are many other people who I have assisted in connecting to their Higher Self whose lives have also been enhanced. I recently received the following from a man whose life has changed dramatically since he connected with his Higher Self four years ago:

"Connecting with my Higher Self has enabled me to combat my ego, which was always screaming messages of fear, inadequacy and scarcity. Before connecting with my Higher Self, I was controlled by my ego most of the time, resulting in unkind and unloving acts to myself — and correspondingly to those around me. With my ego directing my actions, words and thinking, I worked myself mercilessly and insanely at the office and at home, often without justification and often resulting in no real accomplishment. All of this deprived me of precious time with my family. Secondarily, it also deprived me of time to develop other aspects of myself. Connecting with my Higher Self has made it possible to change the way I have always lived my life and I can honestly report I am now living in Joy."

If you desire to receive higher guidance, you will be able to do so when the time is right for you. It may not happen immediately, but it *will* happen when you are truly willing and ready. You may need to let go of some anger first; or, you might need to slow down the pace of your life so you can learn to quiet your mind.

The process of connecting with your Higher Self is not difficult once you have learned to quiet your mind. It is not necessary that your mind be totally clear, for that rarely happens when beginning the Path. All that is necessary is a willingness to try to quiet the mind, and to stay open. Those who have experience with various forms of meditation usually have no difficulty in connecting with Higher Self, and in fact may already have done so. Former experience in quieting your mind is not essential, however. All that is required is the willingness to connect with your Higher Self, and to stay open to what is received.

Some people, such as I, hear a quiet, loving voice. Others have a more visual type of experience, and see images or scenes. Or one may simply experience a sense of deep inner knowingness. For many people, the message is received in the form of their own thoughts. It does not matter. *Your Higher Self will choose the way that can most easily be received by you.*

Messages from your Higher Self are always gentle and loving, regardless of the way in which they are received. They are also patient and very wise. While you may be made aware of truths you have preferred not to see, your Higher Self will place no demands upon you. Instead, wise and loving counsel will be given. It is your choice whether or not to follow this guidance. No matter how many times guidance is refused, loving messages continue if we but ask. If we could only be so loving and so patient with ourselves! But, of course, that is what our Higher Self is trying to teach us — self-love. And as we grow in love for ourselves, we become more gentle and patient with others, and our lives begin to fill with Joy.

A word of warning is necessary here: beware of your ego (the fearful and unloving part of your personality). Ego will sometimes try to pass itself off as your Higher Self, for its intention is to remain in control of your life. If you receive messages that contain fear thoughts or thoughts of scarcity of any kind, or if the message is negative or unloving in any way, then you know you have connected with your ego.

Guidance received from Higher Self is always gentle, loving and wise, and is intended only for healing and spiritual growth. Its purpose is to enhance, not to demean. Ego controls though fear; Higher Self guides and teaches through love. Since fear is but an absence of love, as we become more loving we experience less fear and our ego loses much of its control over our lives. The result is increased Joy.

Guides, Teachers and Angels

It is important to note here that when some people begin making connection to higher guidance, the messages they receive seem to come from a source outside of themselves. Many connect with spiritual beings of great light and love — guides, teachers or angels — who assist human beings in spiritual awakening by offering wise counsel and guidance. As with Higher Self, the messages received are always loving and gentle, and are intended only for personal healing and spiritual growth.

Two years after making connection with my Higher Self, I began receiving occasional messages from another source, who said he was a guide. Since that time I have received guidance from several guides and teachers, in addition to my Higher Self. The messages I receive from my guides and teachers are helpful and pertinent to my daily life, for I have been given much sound advice, and, at times, loving admonishment when I have needed it.

As an example, I will share a recent message now. I was feeling angry at a dear friend. She has a history of serious illness, and I did not feel she was taking care of herself. I received the following message: *"You must not allow fear to contaminate your relationship with your friend. Your anger at her is only your fear of losing her. Do not underestimate her, Dear One, or yourself, for you have great power and influence with her. She is struggling, and needs unconditional love and positive regard from you now."* I took this advice to heart, and my relationship with my friend has deepened.

It is important to remember that *all higher guidance is loving and wise,* regardless of the source of the guidance. And it is also important to remember that each of us is *always at choice*. Follow only guidance which feels loving and right, for it is you who is the orchestrator of your life.

7

CONNECTING WITH HIGHER SELF

Attune yourself to the
wise and loving guidance
of your Higher Self.

Before beginning the process of attempting to connect with your Higher Self, it is necessary to first center yourself, to become totally present in the moment. You are not going to be successful in connecting with your Higher Self if you are thinking about other things. It is necessary to calm your mind, and be totally focused on the process of connecting.

It is helpful to begin by taking several deep breaths. This will begin the process of calming your mind. Next, gently raise your shoulders, lifting them toward your ears, and then bring them down slowly.

Repeat this until you feel relaxed. Ask for the light of God, (or All That Is) to surround and protect you now.

There are many ways to bring our often scattered parts of self together, and begin to focus our mind. As I said before, meditating is an effective way to center and clear the mind. Or, you may prefer to listen to quiet music for several minutes, allowing yourself to relax and focus upon the beauty of the sounds you are hearing. Reading inspiring books or daily affirmations is another way to calm your thoughts. I prefer sitting quietly and going within myself.

In the beginning, when I wanted to connect with my Higher Self, I found it helpful to sit with my back straight and my hands resting quietly in my lap. I would shut my eyes, and visualize myself slowly going down ten steps, one at a time. Beginning with the number ten, I would count each step in my mind as I reached it, and take a deep breath. When I reached number one, I left the final step and visualized myself in a beautiful, safe place — a lovely, green meadow with flowers and butterflies. It was at this point that I would ask for higher guidance. (I now find this process unnecessary.)

Whatever method you choose to use, it is important to take as much time as necessary to calm your thoughts and get yourself ready to meet with your

Higher Self. It may take several attempts at centering yourself before you are successful. You may find it difficult at first to even sit still. Your thoughts may continue to race, even as you are trying to calm them. Do not be discouraged. Learning to slow down the mind — and yourself — is most worthwhile in itself. Many of us live at an almost frantic pace, and learning to slow down may require some practice. But it is well worth the time and effort it takes. Learning to calm our minds is a necessary prerequisite to receiving higher guidance.

Steps To Follow In Connecting With Your Higher Self

When I am assisting someone as they attempt to make their first connection to higher guidance, I ask them to complete the following steps:

(1) Find a quiet place where you will not be interrupted or distracted by other people, ringing telephones, etc. Have a notebook and pen with you. Make the commitment to yourself to sit quietly, and with deep sincerity ask for God's light and love to surround and protect you. (Do not neglect this step). Begin to let your mind clear, using whatever method you prefer. It is often helpful to take several deep breaths, as this will help you to center yourself. Take as much time as you need to relax and open your

mind.

(2) When you are relaxed and feel ready to proceed, close your eyes and imagine that a very wise and very loving Being is present. You can visualize this Being in any way you desire. Sit quietly until you have located this wise Being. See him or her bathed in light, and feel this light beginning to surround you.

(3) Come close to this wise Being and say that you wish to receive guidance. If you have a specific question in mind, ask it now. Make certain it is not a question from your ego, such as, "Will I get the raise I want?" A more appropriate question would be, "How can I be more loving to myself?" If you do not have a question in mind, simply ask, "What do I need to know now?" Wait quietly for an answer, which will probably come in the form of your own thoughts. Simply listen without any judgement, and begin writing what you are hearing (or thinking). You will be amazed at the wealth of knowledge that is within you when you ask for higher guidance.

(4) When you are finished, thank the wise Being or the message you have received. If you heard the guidance, and have written it, read it now. If you received visually or on a feeling level, write as accurately as you can what you experienced.

Do not get discouraged if at first it seems like nothing is happening. You will make connection to higher guidance when you are ready. Simply stay open and continue trying. Your ability to connect with your Higher Self will increase as you practice the above steps.

In order to maximize the positive results that are available to you, make a commitment to yourself to meet with your Higher Self every day. Your ego will try to discourage you, telling you that you do not have time, and you are probably making all of this up, anyway. Do not listen! If the guidance you are receiving is loving and pertinent to your life, you owe it to yourself to meet with your Higher Self on a regular basis. I find it works best for me to make time in the morning before I start the day's routine. Connecting with my Higher Self starts my day on a positive note, and I find I go through the day with less effort, and experience greater Joy.

It is very helpful to write down — and keep — the guidance you receive. Doing so helps imprint it in your mind, making it more easily understood and remembered. Also, the guidance we are given is often so wise and so relevant to our lives that it can prove extremely useful when read again at a later time. I have kept all my writings, and find myself amazed at how much I still learn from them when reading them months, or even years later. Sometimes it takes me that long to be ready to really listen — with my heart as well as my ears. But that is perfectly all right, for our Higher Selves are very patient, and gently continue to tell us what we need to learn (often in many different ways) until such time as we are ready to grow.

8

ACCEPTING PERSONAL POWER

*We each have great
power, for the light of
God shines in us all.*

We create so much of our lives by the thoughts
that we think, and the choices that we make. While
we may like to believe we are victims, in truth we
are not. Yet fully realizing this can be difficult, es-
pecially when we deny our own power. And our ego
(fear) will often tell us we are powerless; that it is
appropriate to be fearful, for the world is a danger-
ous place — and besides, no one could really love us
anyway.

But fear is of ego, and has no place in the lives of
those who choose to walk the Path of Joy. We weaken
ego by challenging its insane and unloving messages
and by acting in love, even as it is warning us not to
do so. *But most of all we weaken ego by taking full*

responsibility for ourselves, our lives and our happiness.

I have found it very difficult to accept the truth that I am the only one responsible for me. For most of my life I preferred feeling responsible for others, hoping that by my taking care of them, they would love me and take care of me. But it never happened that way, and I was often disappointed and angry, feeling I had given so much and received so little in return. As I struggled to change my patterns, my Higher Self supported me with gentle guidance:

"Carla, accepting one's personal power is often terrifying, particularly for those who were forced to give their's away in childhood in order to survive. Accepting personal power means having to give up all the devious ways one previously got one's needs met, such as games, hints, etc. Accepting your personal power means you must take full responsibility for meeting your own needs, which includes telling others what you need from them. It means giving up being a victim. Responsibility for oneself can seem terrifying, but how freeing it is when total responsibility for oneself is taken.

"You have been in the process of taking responsibility for yourself for several years. The process has seemed slow — simply because you had so much to unlearn. It has been difficult for you to separate emotionally from your family of origin, and to sepa-

rate emotionally from your husband. Putting bound-aries around yourself is what we are talking about here, or as your husband said, 'developing a self.' You always had a 'Self', but it has been difficult to recognize it because of all the layers of negative, false learning that covered and surrounded it. Good work, Carla. I am with you always."

How does one fully recognize, accept and utilize personal power? How does one stop playing victim, and begin living in Joy? We begin by accepting the truth that we are much more than we realize. I am more than a body and a personality named Carla. I am a loving being of light, and I am eternal. And so are you. We are here to learn to love, and we can speed up the process by forgiving ourselves our human imperfections even as we strive to correct them. *To accept our personal power, we must first accept ourselves as we now are.* We need to remember we are here to learn, not to be perfect, for perfection is impossible to attain in any facet of ourselves or our lives. We must accept this truth.

It is necessary to take responsibility for our own Joy, and our spiritual growth. We must cease judging ourselves harshly. We must cease blaming others. We must accept that at the core of our Being we are truly wonderful and loving. And we must put this into daily action. We must change the old patterns that were created in fear, and practice *lov-*

ingness. Practice, practice, practice; and forgive ourselves when we fail to remember who we really are, and once again react from fear.

During the years I struggled to change my life and accept my own power, I have learned three important lessons that I would like to share with you. I hope you will find them beneficial as you walk your own Path of Joy.

Lesson One

I Am Not A Body Or A Personality

Discovering that I am neither a body nor a personality is perhaps the most liberating lesson I have learned. For so many years I thought I was both. I was concerned about how I looked, how I dressed, and how I appeared to others. I was a 'people-pleaser' with an attractive body, and I defined myself by the roles I played — wife, mother, sister, psychotherapist, and teacher. Now I realize none of that is who I really am. I have learned we are all so much more than we realize. We have great love and power within us. In truth, we *are* love. Everything else is secondary to that truth.

We cannot be our bodies. It is unthinkable that we are but a physical shell. Yet we often seem to think our bodies are who we are, and we spend incredible amounts of time, effort and money trying to protect, preserve and beautify our physical form. We want to feel good, look good, stay young — we are even concerned with how we smell. Yet regardless of all our efforts, our bodies age and die. We are not bodies, and to think that we are is to be confused. We cannot be our bodies, for we are eternal.

We are also not our personalities — the individual and separate selves the world sees. Our personalities constantly undergo change as we travel through life. I am much different than I was five years ago, and I barely remember the person I was in my twenties. I know there will be more changes in my personality as I continue to learn and grow. Our personalities are not who we are, for we are much, much more.

If we are not our bodies or our personalities, who are we? We are beings of love and light. We are part of God (or All That Is), and we are the creators of our lives. We live as we choose. If we choose love and Joy, we create loving, joyful lives. If we choose fear, we create for ourselves a painful existence. It is as simple as that. Accepting the truth of who we are is highly liberating, for it enables us to consciously choose the path we will travel in life.

Lesson Two

Everything I Seek Is Within Me

The second important lesson I have learned is that everything I have sought from others is inside of me. I realize now it is a complete waste of time to look for love, fulfillment or Joy outside of myself, for it simply cannot be found anywhere but within me. This is true for all of us. We waste our time and give away our power, and our chance to live in Joy by looking for someone or something to complete us — to make us whole. We *are* whole and complete, although few among us recognize this truth.

I have great power. So do you. For so many years I could not see the many ways I allowed my ego (fear) to disempower and disable me. A vital lesson I have learned is that I have the power to create anything that is for my higher good, and that I have the loving support of my Higher Self assisting me to do so. The life I am living now would not have seemed possible even a few short years ago. I feel happier and more alive than ever before. The people who are now in my life love and affirm me, as I do them. I am free to create in any way I choose. And I am manifesting abundance.

Lesson Three

Practicing Self-Love Is Essential

The third significant lesson I have learned in my own life, and from working with clients for many years, is the importance of doing the loving thing for myself at all times. This is not selfish or wrong. To the contrary, it is absolutely essential that we base our actions on what is loving for us. I wholeheartedly believe that when we do the loving thing for ourselves, it is always the loving thing for everyone else, even though this may not seem apparent at the time. Every time I have chosen to do the loving thing for myself, it has ultimately turned out to be the loving thing for the other person (or persons) as well. It is an error in judgment to self-sacrifice if doing so is unloving or unkind to you.

We need to seriously question doing anything that diminishes our Joy. Doing things we do not want to do because we think we should or must rarely turns out to be the loving thing for us — or for the other person. 'Should', 'must' and 'supposed to', are favorite words of our ego (fear), and have no place in the lives of those who walk the Path of Joy. We are doing no one a favor when we give reluctantly because we think we have to, or are supposed to. We need to liberate ourselves from the 'musts' and the 'shoulds', so that we can give freely from love.

I have given up being a 'people-pleaser', and I no longer put others' wants and needs above my own. I make every effort to do the loving thing for myself in all circumstances.

Yet paradoxically, I find I am more loving than ever before, as my husband and children will readily affirm. I give from love, and not from feelings of obligation or responsibility. My gifts come from my heart, and there are no strings attached to them. I find giving from love to be pure Joy.

Begin now to focus the immense love that is within you *on yourself*. Let it fill and permeate your entire being. Make the choice to do the loving thing for yourself at all times and in all situations. If you will do this, your love of others will increase, and you will become a beacon of light to the world.

Our personal power comes only from our loving-ness. It is as simple as that. And the more we act in love towards ourselves and others, the greater our personal power. So the choice that must be made is love, for in this world of illusion, *love is the only real power.*

EPILOGUE

BE PATIENT WITH YOURSELF

*Change occurs more easily when
accompanied by loving patience.
Remember, you are on no time but God's.*

I am on a beautiful tropical island as I write this
book, and I am practicing living in Joy. Yet even
here, where I am surrounded by incredible beauty
and am with my husband, who I love above all others, I still manage at times to stray from the Path.
It is as though I can only allow myself so much Joy
before I find a way to end it. My Higher Self re-
minds me to be patient, and helps me to see how I
strayed off the Path (usually it is because I have
given into ego). We must be very patient with ourselves as we learn to change our unhappy patterns
and live our lives more joyfully.

Why do we choose pain instead of Joy? Why do we sabotage our own happiness? Why do we react in anger, rather than respond in love? Why, even after we have made the connection to our Higher Self, do we sometimes stray from the Path of Joy?

While one can name many reasons, the truth is it is not because of our unhappy childhood, difficult partner, bad mood or the difficulties we experience in our daily lives. It is because the vast majority of us have not yet recognized that Joy is our birthright, and our natural state. It seems we are far more familiar with misery. It is amazing how adept we are at sabotaging our happiness, no matter how loudly we proclaim otherwise. Our egos are masters at stopping Joy, and we often allow it, however unwittingly.

We stray from the Path of Joy whenever we allow our ego (fear) to control us. Be patient and gentle with yourself when this happens. Forgive yourself when you react from fear, rather than respond from love. Remember, changing old patterns takes time. Simply persevere. You *will* learn to live in Joy. This will happen more easily if you make time every day to nurture yourself, and to meet with your Higher Self.

My life is very different now, and I am experiencing a deeper level of satisfaction and contentment than I ever thought possible. I am more loving and patient with myself than ever before, and because of this, I am more loving and patient with everyone else. Love liberates and heals. Love *is* Joy. And we are all worthy of Joy, each and every one of us.

It is my prayer that this book will be of help to all who are seeking a more loving and more joyous way of life. I hope that you, too, will choose to walk the Path of Joy, and awaken to the glorious truth of who you are. You are light and love, and your presence in the world is needed now.

ABOUT THE AUTHOR

Carla A. Nelson is a Licensed Clinical Social Worker with many years experience as a psychotherapist. She taught at the University of Kentucky, and has recently retired from private practice in order to devote her time to writing and conducting workshops. She has two grown children, and lives with her husband and three cats on an island in the Bahamas, where she is practicing living in Joy.